push it guys

When my body shouts ‘STOP’, my mind screams ‘NEVER’.

HESCO
2941

ESCO
519
NEFROG

APEX

HESCO
25340
BONEFROG

EST:MMXI

SPARTAN RACE
OCR

HESCO

FROG ELITE

HYLETE

FROG ELITE

BONE FROG

21686

27812

COMPRESSION

live to die

Hebrews 13:5

784

USA

HESCO
27665
BONEFROG

GOT AFTER

FROG ELITE

BONEFROG

USA
WRESTLING
Navy

Family First

ESCO
519
NEFROG

FROG ELITE
BONEFROG

HESCO
25383
BONEFROG

BONE

HESCO
25340
BONEFROG

XT46

Fidelis

EST:MMXII

teslagears

Navy SEAL
3489
BONEFROG

RYU
RESPECT YOUR

FROG ELITE

HESCO
25462
BONEFROG

USA
5

USA

BL CK
THOUGHT

GOT AFTER IT

Family
First

XT46

27812

BEAST
HESCO
27260
BONEFROG

BONEFROG
HESCO
27752
BONEFRO

BONEFROG
HESCO
27284
BONEFROG

FROG ELITE
CATERPY

HESCO

27665

3711

EST:MMXII

Family
First

UNITED
CORPS

FIT

#LOVEMUD

Patriot

HESCO
27116
BONEFROG
adidas

#LOVEMUD

NAVY SEAL

BO
NAVY S

#LOVEMUD

CPSIA information can be obtained
at www.ICGtesting.com
Printed in the USA
BVHW050820220719
554056BV00025B/1794/P

9 780464 049753